WHAT'S IT LIKE TO BE A...?

GAME DEVELOPER

Elizabeth Dowen **Lisa Thompson**

First published in the UK 2009 by
A & C Black Publishing Ltd
36 Soho Square
London
W1D 3QY
www.acblack.com

Copyright © 2009 Blake Publishing
Published by Black Education Pty Ltd, Australia

ISBN: 978-1-4081-1422-3

A CIP catalogue record for this book is available from the British Library.

Written by Lisa Thompson and Elizabeth Dowen
Publisher: Katy Pike
Editor: Eve Tonelli
Cover Design: Terry Woodley
Designer: Matt Lin and Clifford Hayes
Printed in Singapore by Tien Wah Press.

Cover image © Shutterstock.

All inside images © Shutterstock except p. 22 and p. 23 Playstation images
courtesy of Sony Computer Entertainment Australia.

This book is produced using paper made from wood grown in managed,
sustainable forests. It is natural, renewable and recyclable. The logging and
manufacturing processes conform to the environmental regulations of the
country of origin.

All the Internet addresses given in this book were correct at the time of
going to press. The author and publishers regret any inconvenience caused
if addresses have changed or sites have ceased to exist, but can accept no
responsibility for any such changes.

Contents

Games, games and more games

Maybe it's time to tidy up a bit.

Everywhere I look, I am surrounded by games. My corner of the office is covered in game design books, game demos, cover art and proposals that my team and I are working on.

As a game developer, I am thinking, writing, playing or talking about games for most of the day, and while finished games can be a lot of fun, getting there involves hard work and long hours!

Everyone's working hard.

Starting with a strong idea is so important.

CONCEPT ORIGINAL SOLUTION
RESPONSE + IMAGINATION
TASK - GIVEN FORM
IMAGINATION + RATIONALITY

TURN ON

My latest project is top secret. We are developing a new game called *Level 11*. It is still in the early stages, but I'm excited about the direction the game is taking. I've got a busy time ahead of me over the next few months!

DID YOU KNOW?

Nintendo began life in the late 19th century as a maker of card games.

What does a game developer do?

A game developer is a person who makes computer games. Developers create the concept, layout and game design. Game developers work out the aim of the game, the rules of play and the look of the game. They decide what it's about, how it looks and sounds, the lot!

rough ideas

Being a developer involves a lot of thinking.

Every game developer dreams of coming up with a game that explores new areas and is original and compelling.

Ideas go from my notepad to my computer.

Game consoles are popular now.

Game on

Digital and electronic games can be played on different platforms:

- computers
- televisions with attached game consoles, such as Sony *PlayStation*, Microsoft *Xbox*, Nintendo *Wii*
- hand-held game consoles, like Nintendo's *DS*, Sony's *PSP* and Apple's *iPod Touch*
- PDAs (Personal Digital Assistants – handheld computers)
- mobile phones
- arcade machines.

People can play games on their PDAs.

He's gaming on his mobile.

Arcade Mania

Arcade Mania

Arcade games – where it all started!

5

HOW I BECAME A GAME DEVELOPER

Studying at uni really developed my skills.

I have always played games for fun. At university, I studied computer science and I made my first game for an assignment. I had a group of friends who liked playing games, and that's pretty much all we would talk about. I was either playing games or looking at books on how to design games.

I got a part-time job testing games for a games-development company near the university. There wasn't a lot of money involved, but I hoped the experience would lead somewhere.

Eventually, it did. One day, when I was in my final year of study, they were really busy and asked me to write some copy for an educational game they were working on.

DID YOU KNOW?

There's no guarantee a game will sell.

WHEN GAMES GO BAD

This is where I work.

In 1982, the Atari company released an *E.T. the Extra-Terrestrial* video game, based on the movie of the same name. It is considered to be the worst video game ever and was a huge flop. Rumour has it that Atari buried thousands of the unsold game cartridges in a New Mexico desert landfill.

After that, my boss invited me to sit in on some development meetings when they were thrashing out game ideas. I enjoyed coming up with game ideas and trying to invent new styles of gameplay.

In meetings, I listened carefully then tried to bring new ideas to the table . . .

When I finished university, I landed a full-time job with the company and I have been with them for three years now. I guess my best piece of advice for anyone who really wants to work in the games industry is play, play, play – and try to build on and improve the games you enjoy.

. . . and that's how I managed to get a full-time job.

You never know, you might come up with a totally new and highly addictive game – every game developer's dream!

CULTURE VULTURES
Computer games are so popular now that gamers have their own culture – they discuss games and share tips in online forums and in virtual communities. Many universities and colleges even have gaming social clubs.

It's another world!

What is a game?

Games are rule-based, interactive play. Games often involve challenge or conflict and are designed to have a defined outcome.

VIDEO GAMES CAN BE DIVIDED INTO FIVE MAIN CATEGORIES

1. ACTION GAMES

Including:
- arcade shooting games, e.g. *Space Invaders*
- first-person and third-person shooters, e.g. *Doom* and *Tomb Raider*
- stealth games, e.g. *Metal Gear*
- dancing games, e.g. *Dance Factory*
- action-adventure games, e.g. *The Legend of Zelda*
- platform games, e.g. *Sonic the Hedgehog*.

2. STRATEGY / WAR GAMES

Including:
- real-time strategy and tactics games, e.g. *Dune II* and *Close Combat*
- turn-based strategy and tactics games, e.g. *Civilization* and *Jagged Alliance*
- management games, e.g. *SimCity*, where players are rulers of their own world.

You have to plan ahead and consider different options in these games.

3. SIMULATIONS

Including:
- sport simulations, e.g. football or golf games like *World Tour Golf*
- vehicle simulations, such as driving games, e.g. *Gran Turismo*, and submarine simulators, e.g. *Dangerous Waters*.

stealth game in progress

Dancing games are popular now.

Now that's action ... and adventure!

Ever wanted to pilot a fighter jet?

4. ADVENTURE GAMES

Including:

- text-based adventures, e.g. *Cities of Glory*
- graphical adventures, e.g. *Torin's Passage.*

5. ROLE-PLAYING GAMES

Including:

- turn-based, role-playing games, e.g. the *Final Fantasy* series
- massively multiplayer, role-playing games, e.g. *World of Warcraft.*

You can be a dragon slayer ... or a dragon!

TOP 5 GAME GENRES

1. **First-person shooters**
   The goal is simple and constant. The player sees the action through the eyes of an avatar and fires the hero's weaponry at just about anything that moves.
2. **Real-time strategies**
   The key to these games is usually balancing defence and attack. They offer the player more than one way of approaching each battle. These games require the ability to plan ahead and predict consequences.

first-person shooter

3. **Sports games**
   These games follow the rules of real-life sports, like golf or skiing.
4. **Puzzles**
   Problem solving skills are key for these games, such as *Minesweeper* or *Bejewelled*.
5. **Role-playing games**
   Players take on the role of an adventurer and go on a series of quests that lead to the story's conclusion.

sports games

9

Skills
NEEDED TO BE A
GAME DEVELOPER

- ◆ excellent computer skills
- ◆ wide knowledge and understanding of computer games
- ◆ creativity and imagination
- ◆ problem-solving skills
- ◆ patience and attention to detail
- ◆ flexibility and adaptability
- ◆ good teamwork and communication skills
- ◆ ability to work under pressure and meet deadlines
- ◆ willingness to keep up with industry developments

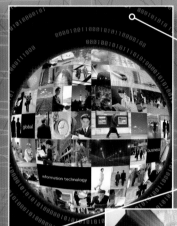

computer skills and knowledge

Patience please!

SKILL UP

Being a game developer involves lots of writing, so it is important to have as much writing experience as possible. Graphic design and programming skills also help developers to understand visual and technical possibilities and to discover new areas to explore.

Don't get left behind.

Start early.

Graphic design will transform your ideas into reality.

DIDYOUKNOW?

Computer game developers earn in the range of £21,500 – £27,000 a year, rising to £33,500 – £43,000. Higher earners can make around £52,000 a year.

Game design

The process of game design can be broken down into a series of steps.

We're only limited by our imaginations.

STEP 1 IMAGINE A GAME
What is the big idea or high concept?
What is your game about?
What type of game is it? (action-adventure, role-playing etc.)
What are the goals for the player?

Lots of games come from the real world too.

STEP 2 HOW WILL THE GAME WORK?
- What are the rules?
- How will it become more difficult?
- What will end the game?

STEP 3 DESCRIBE THE GAME ASPECTS
- What is the setting?
- How many characters does it have?
- What special features will it contain?
- What will it look like?

THE GAME IDEA
Ideas for games come from four main sources:
- original ideas – brand new ideas of possible worlds, characters and stories
- other media – films, TV, literature, music, popular culture
- other games – improving on existing games and adding to popular games
- the real world – games inspired by real life.

STEP 4 DOCUMENTING THE DESIGN
- What is the blueprint for the game's development?

A blueprint is a set of guidelines that defines the game. These are written by the game developer for the team to follow. It is the developer's role to produce a clear and comprehensive guide to the game.

11

Elements of game design

One of the first questions a game developer needs to ask when designing a new game is: "What is the goal of the game?"

Collecting trophies is always fun.

POSSIBLE GOALS

- save something/someone, e.g. a princess locked in a tower
- find something, e.g. an ancient, lost treasure
- play as long as possible to achieve the highest score
- successfully finish a series of levels
- defeat other players/characters

DIDYOUKNOW?

Only around 20% of games make a profit, whilst 40% are likely to draw even.

Slushy the Snowman has to ski 10 levels!

FIRST OUTLINE THE BASICS OF THE GAME:

- the goal of the game
- the game's intended audience
- the genre of the game
- the game's unique selling points.

Once the goal of the game is understood, there are three key building areas of the game:

1 **rules**
2 **story**
3 **interaction.**

The rule book sets out the limits of the game.

RULES

Rules are the formal structure of the game. Some general characteristics that all games share are:

- rules limit player action
- rules are clear and easy to understand
- rules are shared by all players
- rules are fixed
- rules are binding
- rules are repeatable.

The rules of any game can be divided into three types.

CONSTITUTIVE RULES are the mathematical rules of a game. These rules are the building blocks that create the game, such as the sky will be blue, or each character will have four eyes.

OPERATIONAL RULES are the "rules of play" that players follow when playing the game. These rules are the actual rules of how to play, e.g. you have to take turns, or you can only jump when you're on the trampoline etc.

These are the rules we're all familiar with — how fast can I run, how many barrels do I have to collect to move onto the next level?

IMPLICIT RULES are the "unwritten rules" of good and fair behaviour that should be understood when a game is played, e.g. to not use rude or aggressive language.

STORY

The story is what drives the game. The story contributes to the look, feel and pace of the game.

Stories can be as simple as jumping obstacles to get to the other side of a river, or as difficult as following multiplayer narratives.

It all begins with an outline for the story. The player's actions affect the way the story unfolds. Designers develop the outline into a complex script showing the options a player might take and the consequences, leading to different conclusions.

So the player has to finish all those tasks and then jump ...

Simple or complex, for the game to work, the story must both convince players to play the game and hold their attention once they're playing. There must also be a series of obstacles that will have two or more outcomes.

That wasn't the outcome he was hoping for.

You want to get to the city, but the maze is blocking your way. So you have to find your way through it. And there's your game.

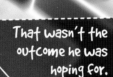

Follow the steps.

To do this, designers use tools such as flowcharts, storyboards and index cards. Many of these tools are available as computer programs. Eventually, a final script for the entire game has been developed.

WANT	+	OBSTACLE	=	ACTION
(goal)		(challenges blocking the goal)		(outcomes for the player)

Name: Emma Dunne
Occupation: Game tester
Basically, I play games all day, pushing them to their limits – and beyond. My job is not as easy as you might think. I have to find bugs in a game, and then reproduce them. I backtrack every step I've taken and try to narrow it down to the essential things that trigger the bug.

Problem-solving and deduction abilities are crucial to being able to quickly route out a bug and then report it to the programmer or developer to fix it.

If you want to be a tester, you have to really love playing video games, because you might be playing the same game every day for six months! To get it right, you might be playing the same level of the same game for weeks. The trick is to find new ways to approach the game so you don't get bored.

You must be able to stay on target.

The worst part of the job is when you end up tracking a single bug for hours and hours. You want to give up, but you have to keep going. Game testing requires lots of patience and can be tedious.

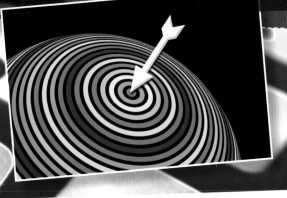

Who?
What?
Where?
When?
Why?
How?

In the video game world Shigeru Miyamoto is a genius. He is the inventor of games such as *Mario*, *Donkey Kong*, *Zelda* and *Nintendogs*. Miyamoto has said he likes the idea of creating games a grandchild and a grandparent can play together, and he has managed to achieve exactly that.

INTERACTIO

Developers need to ask themselves a series of questions about player interaction, such as –

- What kind of players is th game aimed at?
- What will the game look a sound like?
- Is the game in the 1st pers or 3rd person?
- Does the player assume th role of an avatar?
- Do players play with othe If so, how?
- What is the heart of the gameplay – speed, action, style – is it continuous, turn-based etc?
- How much control will the player have?

SELECT YOUR CHARACTER

CHALLENGES, GAMEPLAY AND VICTORY

Gameplay is a general term for the series c challenges that face a player as they play Developers create the rules that define thes challenges. They need to think about the num and complexity of different challenges for different levels.

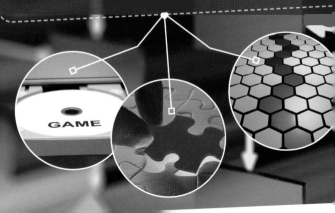

GAME

Well, it looks like the game is pretty enjoyable.

Developers may also want to incorporate minigames, a short game contained within the bigger game. They provide different challenges in a game and a break from the main story.

Once demos of a level have been made, testing is done to see if the challenges, gameplay and victory conditions make the game enjoyable and fulfil the player's expectations.

But I want to win!

Most games have a special kind of rule that defines the victory condition. The victory condition is when a player has won the game – but not all games can be won. Shaping victory and loss conditions are an important part of successful game design.

A decision tree is a diagram that maps out all the possible decisions and outcomes in a game. They help developers understand how players move through the game and the possible endings.

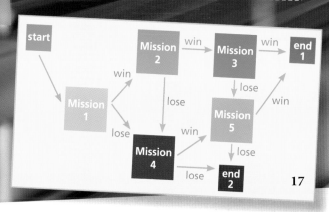

17

What is Level 11?

Let's take a look . . .

LEVEL 11 – AN OVERVIEW
First-person combat

Level 11 is a doorway into 11 layered monster worlds. Each level is a different environment containing a particular monster that must be found and killed. Each monster can only be killed with a particular piece of weaponry that players also have to find.

As the player progresses through the levels, they become more and more dangerous. Monsters from previous levels appear and the environments become more complex. Players must use multiple combat applications to survive.

For me, this is one of the most exciting parts of developing a game – choosing between all the possibilities. I'm imagining how all the different levels will look, the sound of the creatures as they roar and how to make the game interesting and fun to play. We've got some great monsters lined up!

It's time to get started.

Watch out for the basilisk!

18

the Cernwennan dagger

LEVEL	MONSTER	WEAPON
1	Hellhound	Durendal sword
2	Golem	Cernwennan dagger
3	Troll	Gáe Bulg spear
4	Ghoul	Sudar disc
5	Demon	Mjolnir hammer
6	Centaur	Zeus' thunderbolt
7	Griffin	golden mace
8	Minotaur	Fragarach sword
9	Basilisk	Fire javelin
10	Gorgon	Gandiva bow
11	Kraken	Kusanagi sword

the Fragarach sword

a golden mace

the Gáe Bulg spear

a centaur

I created this demon.

Our troll is pretty fierce.

cool griffin

Get started online.

DID YOU KNOW?

NET HELP

There are lots of tools available online for building games. Some require basic programming skills, but others are easier and allow you to build a game with only a little technical knowledge.

The PS3 has a game called *LittleBigPlanet*, offering a set of tools to design game levels of your own, and upload them for others to play. You design the specifics of the game and can fill it with photos and music of your choice.

19

A history of video games

It is important for game developers to have a good understanding of the history of video game design and key moments in game evolution.

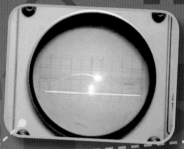

It was called *Tennis for Two*.

1962

START HERE

1958

1958
Physicist William Higinbotham invents the first video game in New York — a tennis-like game played on a machine called an oscilloscope.

1962
First interactive computer game, *Spacewar!*, created by university student Steve Russell.

1978

1980 < KEEP GOING

1978
Space Invaders, the first game to track and display high scores, is launched into arcades.

1980
The first 3-D arcade game, *Battlezone*, is created by Atari. Set on a virtual battlefield, it is used by the US Government for training exercises.

It was a tank game.

The arcade game *Pac-Man* is released worldwide by Namco. An alternative to the other space shooter arcade games, it becomes one of the most famous games of all time.

You must recognise *Pac-Man*!

Defender, the first arcade game using a virtual world, is introduced.

the famous *Pong*

1970
Nolan Bushnell and Ted Dabney create an arcade version of *Spacewar!*, called *Computer Space* – the first video arcade game.

1972
Bushnell and Dabney start the Atari company.

THIS

WAY >

1970

1972

1975

a *Computer Space* arcade machine

1975
Atari make 150,000 home consoles of the table tennis-like game *Pong*. It becomes the hottest Christmas present that year.

an original Atari 2600

1977
Atari launches the first cartridge-based home computer system, the *Atari 2600*. Games can now be bought separately and played through the console.

1977

laserdisc   CD   mini-CD

1981
Nintendo brings out arcade game *Donkey Kong* – the first platform game that allows players to jump over obstacles and gaps.

1981

Dragon's Lair arcade game is released – the first game to feature laserdisc technology.

REST HERE

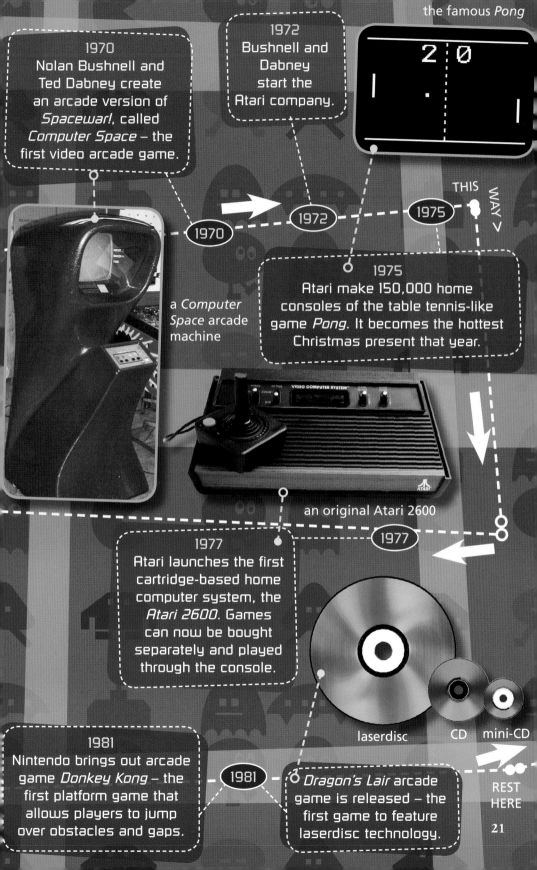

1985
The popular puzzle game *Tetris* is developed by Russian programmer Alex Pajitnov. Originally played on computers, but now available for almost every format (hand-held consoles, mobile phones etc.).

1985

START HERE

an original *Game Boy*

1991
Nintendo brings out the *Super NES*.

1986 **1991**

1986
Nintendo releases the hand-held *Game Boy*.

PlayStation in your pocket

2004

2001

2004
Sony's *PSP* (*PlayStation Portable*) and Nintendo's *DS* go on sale.

2001
Microsoft and Nintendo introduce their next-generation systems within days of each other – Microsoft's *Xbox*, and Nintendo's *Game Boy Advance*.

2005
Microsoft releases the *Xbox 360*, which allows players to compete online, download games, trailers, TV shows and movies.

2005

2006

2006
Nintendo's *Wii* is launched. It has a wireless controller.

1993
The PC game *Doom* is launched. It has groundbreaking graphics and networked multiplayer gaming.

1994
In Japan, the Sega *Saturn* and the Sony *PlayStation* both hit the market.

1995
PlayStation is the most popular game console with 20 million sold.

1993 — 1994

1995

a *PlayStation* console

1996

2000

2000
The Sims comes out, and by 2002, becomes the best-selling PC game ever. With no defined goals, players create virtual people and control their lives and environments.

1996
Nintendo begins selling the *Nintendo 64* in Japan.

The *Tamagotchi* virtual pet becomes an instant sensation.

The *Wii* takes wireless fun to a whole new level.

STOP HERE

Sony bring out *PlayStation 3*.

PLAYSTATION 1, 2, 3 — BIGGER, FASTER, STRONGER
Each generation of PlayStation has built upon the foundations of the one before, with improved graphics, sound, speed, functions and storage capabilities.

The first PlayStation was CD based. The PlayStation 2 was DVD based. The PlayStation 3 has a new media format called Blu-ray, which supports high definition video and has more storage capability than DVD.

23

How many more *PlayStations* will there be?

Who's who in the game-building team

Development teams vary according to the size of a company and the game being produced. Our company is quite small, but we still have different members of the team performing specialised roles.

Chris is in charge of *Level 11*.

Maria's our head programmer for this project.

GAME PRODUCER

Game producers are responsible for the game as a whole. They look at the big picture and are responsible for setting deadlines for coordination and marketing. As a game developer, I work closely with the producer to set realistic targets and make sure the team meets them.

LEAD PROGRAMMER/ PROGRAMMER

The lead programmer heads up a team of programmers in creating the tools for the art and sound. They develop the game's structure that produces the game's functions, graphics and sound.

Peter, a programmer

My partner, Aash, takes a break from writing code.

GAME DEVELOPERS

Developers are often programmers, who create the computer code to make each new game. They may have additional responsibilities, like I do, such as managing other team members, or working on whole games in smaller companies.

LEVEL DESIGNERS

Level or "mission" designers create the structure of the game's missions or levels and fill them with objects, goals and enemies. They work with me as well as with the programmers and artists.

Suki's working on sunsets at the moment.

ARTISTS AND ANIMATORS

In our team, each artist or animator has a specialised role in character, texture or background creation. They create the look of the game.

Lisa is researching colours and textures for the backgrounds.

WRITERS

Writers work closely with the developers to work on the story and dialogue, as well as tutorials and other text that may accompany the game.

Paul thinks about the game's introduction.

SOUND DESIGNERS

Sound designers are responsible for all the sounds that appear in the game. As sounds create mood and character and atmosphere, they need to be able to create their own sounds as well as use libraries and other resources.

Charlie's sorting out monster screams right now.

QUALITY ASSURANCE TESTER

The quality assurance tester checks playability and reliability. They are responsible for reporting problems and bugs.

Developing communication

Keep focused on the target audience.

As a game developer, it's my job to have a clear vision of what the game will be like when it's finished. That's why my job is most intense at the pre-production stage, making sure the team are on target from the start.

This is not the way to communicate!

Game developers rarely create a game alone. So documenting the game's design and keeping the team aware of changes is crucial. It is very important to have constant communication with other sections of the development team.

My job includes making sure everyone understands the game's look, feel and function. The team must communicate well to make changes and deal with problems quickly and effectively.

Any questions?

It's about getting everyone moving in the right direction.

Often, big changes to a game need to happen, and it is the developer's job to explain the changes and the reasons behind them. Game design is as much about communicating ideas as it is about coming up with them.

One of our programmers, Abi, takes a moment to consider some changes.

The UK has a small but thriving computer games industry, and skilled people are in demand. There are also opportunities to work in France, the USA and Japan, where many computer games companies are based.

DOOM

The game *Doom*, released in 1993, kick-started the *first-person shooter* genre. An estimated 10 million people downloaded it within two years. Its lifelike environment, sounds and the new perspective changed the look and feel of gaming.

The game was so addictive, some players suffered *Doom*-induced motion sickness and would vomit after spending hours at their computer screen, while other people actually passed out.

A good developer has a broad understanding of the different areas involved in creating the game, so they understand the possible problems and can offer suggestions and solutions.

Designing thesettingsand characters

Getting an idea for the look of a game is often vital for success.

At the very early concept stage, artists will often work with the developer and come up with sketches for environments and characters. Storyboarding is a useful way to work out how the characters will move through a world.

We considered having a dragon in the game ... then decided against it.

This basilisk is definitely in!

an example of a storyboard

Artists will also come up with a range of colours, tones and moods for the game. The visual feel can define a game just as much as the control system or level layout.

This game has a strong cartoon feel.

I'm thinking of a dark, stormy set of colours.

SEEING IS BELIEVING

A game's environment is extremely important. Effects such as reflections, shadows, surface shine and cloud patterns all contribute to making an environment appear more convincing.

It can be tricky to make clouds look real.

How about an abandoned church for one level?

We throw around ideas for *Level 11*. All ideas and suggestions are documented. Each person shares their thoughts about the game and where they are at with their part of the project.

The artists present some rough sketches for the monster characters, settings and perspective. The writers discuss dialogue for different levels and the sound designers play sounds they think will create a unique atmosphere.

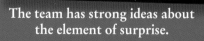
The team has strong ideas about the element of surprise.

one of our many pre-production meetings

IN THE ZONE

Games need to be challenging enough so that they do not bore players, but not so challenging that players get frustrated. It's not easy to find the right balance so that players will enjoy the game and its challenges.

We set to work on producing a demo of the game and the producer and I discuss deadlines for various stages of the project.

GAMING FEATURES SPECIAL

No, not this kind of egg!

LUCKY FOR SOME
Roughly translated from Japanese, Nintendo means "leave luck to heaven".

There have been two major developments in gaming recently:

1. The Internet, and online multi-player gaming
Gamers can now access the Internet through PCs and through portals such as Xbox Live, and play against one another or in teams.

2. Wireless platforms
The new generation of mobile phones and other handheld gaming devices have opened up a market for wireless-transmitted interactive games.

EASTER EGGS
Some games contain secret, hidden messages, images or locations known as Easter eggs. The first Easter egg was created for the Atari 2600 game *Adventure*. Easter eggs are now a standard part of most games.

In the beginning, gamers stumbled across random keystrokes or mouse clicks that made a secret animation appear or a hidden room accessible. Now, there are websites to help gamers discover these special features.

So, if you push the second and fourth levers down, what happens?

Who knew that secret chamber was there?

CHEAT CODES

Cheat codes are button combinations or control sequences which allow players to advance to a hidden level or perform moves that cannot be defeated.

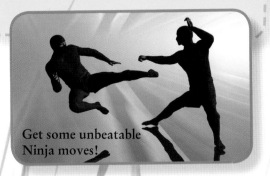

Get some unbeatable Ninja moves!

DOOM LADEN

Doom was one of the first games to gain a large modification-making community. The ability to create custom levels and modify the game was a very popular aspect to the game's original appeal and success.

Doom is set on the planet Mars.

MODIFICATIONS

Modifications (mods) are enhancements or additions that are added to a game. Mods can be new tools, characters, settings, levels, music, story-lines etc. Mods can be made by the developer or the general public. Mods add to the success and life of the game by adding interest and extending the replay value of the game.

Mods change the game and keep it new and fun.

DIDYOUKNOW?

EGG HUNT

Gaming Easter eggs were named after the famous Russian Fabergé eggs. Styled on real Easter eggs, Fabergé eggs were made of precious

LEVELDESIGN

A level designer is responsible for creating each level's own game world – building the environment, placing every object and deciding its purpose. The level designer sets out the enemy's route, how fast they move and the best place to pick up time bonuses. They make sure the players never hit an unintended dead end.

Here's an example of a level – cool spaceship!

These designers must create hidden paths to coax players through the world – without the players realising it.

CREATING MOODS AND FEELINGS
Level designers must also create the feelings of suspense, anticipation and victory in a game. Players should often feel like they're about to run out of time or supplies, but rarely fall short completely.

How many have I got left?

Designers learn how to place packs, water reserves or checkpoints just within reach, but far enough away so the player is bracing themselves for "Game Over". A smart level designer tweaks, tries and tweaks again until the game has the right mix of surprise, thrills and victory.

She didn't see that coming!

Races need fast AND slow parts.

PACING

Level designers control a game's pace so that it is not too boring or slow, but also not too intense all the time. Games need to have both calmer moments, then build up to excitement – such as in racing games, where designers must create track surprises but also the underlying rhythm of the track.

ADVENTURE

In third-person adventure games, the designer places visual clues to show players which parts of the level they can reach to keep them interested and playing the game.

WORLDWIDE KNOWLEDGE

The best game developers have a broad range of interests and knowledge in –
• mathematics
• logic
• history
• literature
• art
• science
• current affairs.

CHARACTERS COME TO LIFE

We need to turn ideas into real graphics.

PROGRESS MEETING WITH THE ART AND PRODUCTION TEAM

Rough sketches are finalised and scanned into the computer where they become controllable 3D characters. The designers then begin to bring the characters to life by defining the characters' shape with control points. These control points will guide the movement of the character when it is in motion.

the art team

These are control points.

Next, the designers add skin, colours and surface texture to the character. Finally, the programmers and designers work together to give the character the ability to move.

Our troll needs to look real.

For super realistic movement, human actors are filmed wearing special suits with sensors that represent the control points of the character's skeleton. These movements are then transferred to the animated character.

setting up to film actors' movements

The game's character can move now.

GAMING CHITCHAT

Gamers have developed their own vocabulary.

noob   'newbie' = someone who is new to
         gaming and asks silly or obvious questions
Leet   written language using keyboard characters
         to communicate over the Internet
über   biggest/most powerful
pwn   'own' = to have outplayed someone else
         in a game, e.g. 'You just got pwned!'

It's a whole new lingo.

PROGRESS MEETING WITH THE SOUND TEAM

Games can require hundreds of individual sound effects. As there are 11 monsters in *Level 11*, we ask the sound designer to provide sound samples for each monster to inspire the art team.

a voice artist at work

Each monster will need a variety of sounds, for when undisturbed, surprised, angry, for its fighting screams, and so on. The sound team and I talk about how we will create some of the stranger monster sounds. We'll need to get creative!

The sound designer also needs to build different sounds for different levels. Gamers understand the power of music. When the music goes quiet, they know they are in trouble.

DESIGNDOCUMENTATION

Now that we have a clear understanding of the goals, gameplay, look and feel of the game, it is time to lock it all into one design document called the Blueprint book. This book is a map of the project for everyone on the team.

Get it all down.

While there is no single structure for game design documents, there are some things which are always included.

Share the vision!

Level 11

A game for PC

1. Brief description of the game (2–4 pages)
The brief description should explain the most basic ideas of the game. For example, *Level 11* is a third-person shooter game in which players must find a specific weapon to kill a monster on each of the 11 levels.

Does the game rely on luck?

That's obviously an action game.

How hard do we make it to land the plane successfully?

2. Game treatment (10–20 pages)

A treatment is a broad outline that lists the basic ideas and aspects of gameplay. It addresses things like:

- What is the planned perspective – 1st person or 3rd person?
- What is the structure – levels, chapters, challenges?
- What is the heart of the gameplay – speed, action, puzzles?
- Will there be a multi-player function?
- How difficult is the game?
- How long will it take the average player to complete?

3. Game script (50–200 pages)

This is a detailed account of how the game will work. It covers all aspects of the game, creative and technical, such as –

- who is the gamer's character?
- a list of the characters in the game and a description of their personalities, capabilities and how they act in the game
- how the different levels are set out
- a detailed structure of the game
- a full description of the style of the graphics, outlining the mood, tone and palette.

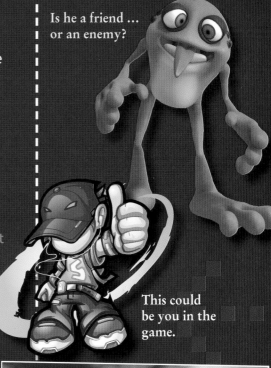

Is he a friend … or an enemy?

This could be you in the game.

choosing the environment

a Wild West setting

TESTING AND TWEAKING

As we develop the game, it is tried out by game testers and our own quality assurance testers who search for bugs and glitches. Developers, like me, must expect to make changes and learn how to compromise without sacrificing the quality of the game.

Adjustments are always needed.

Testers play each level, pushing the game as far as they can. They identify and prioritise bugs and glitches to be fixed.

Bugs can range from minor art glitches to major crash bugs. Generally, bugs can be divided into four categories.

- **A-class bugs** – cause the game to crash or lock up. This category also includes bugs that cause installation failure or features that do not function.

- **B-class bugs** – include graphic glitches such as scenery pop-up or frame-rate issues.

- **C-class bugs** – are spelling errors or minor graphic or audio glitches.

- **D-class bugs** – are usually suggestions, rather than bugs, such as an unappealing colour scheme or texture.

It's all about getting people to buy the game.

Over the past 30 years, video games have become a huge part of our culture, and video games are now a multi-billion pound industry. Successful games often produce related merchandise, like toys and T-shirts.

Level 11 is released

Finally, the game is finished and launched. It's monster madness. Posters and demos are everywhere. Some people have already found the secret levels. Gamers buy it off the Internet or in stores.

There's a happy customer.

Depending on the level of success of *Level 11*, there is talk amongst the production team about doing more *Level* games. I'm already jotting down ideas and thinking about improved gaming strategies and challenges.

That's the life of a game developer – playing the game never stops!

What's the next big thing?

MONEY SPINNER

A cyberathlete is a professional gamer (pro) that plays games for money. A cyberathlete differs from a hardcore gamer because they make money from gaming. So it becomes their job, and they are no longer playing the games

1 Important school subjects will be English, and maths. Computing and art/design skills are also important. A Diploma in Creative Media would also be useful (England). For course entry qualifications speak to your careers teacher/adviser or Connexions PA.

Go keyboard crazy.

2 To work as a games developer, artist or programmer you usually need a relevant BTEC HND or degree.

Art skills will help.

3 Many colleges and universities in the UK offer courses in game design or development or related degrees such as computer science, software engineering, animation, graphic design, maths or physics or interactive media.

Steps to becoming a game developer

4 After gaining your qualification you will usually learn
  on the job from experienced staff. You start at
  junior level and work with the lead designer, artist
  or programmer.

5 Find inspiration on the web. Check out sites with simple
  games like *Space Invaders* and download their files
  to study how they are built. Create your own mod or
  small game.

6 Play, play, play. Play as many different games as you
  can. Study games you like and think about why you like
  playing them and what their strengths and weaknesses
  are. Invent new rules. Brainstorm ideas with friends.

7 Stay up to date with new software packages
  and developments by using the web. Read industry
  magazines, attend gaming conferences and keep up
  to date with various blogs that developers keep on
  the internet.

8 Working as a Game Tester can be a good starting
  point. No qualifications are needed. You need to be
  an avid games player and willing to play games all day,
  testing a game for 3 months or longer and sometimes
  working long hours (which is the case for a lot of jobs
  in this industry).

Employers will want to see proof of your
talent and creativity. Collect a portfolio of
your work including game projects, ideas
for games, artwork, or a 'showreel' CD
or DVD of animation work. This shows
employers you are motivated and teaches
you important skills about problem solving
and the development process.

Other related areas to consider:

The computer games industry is growing and there are many games-related careers available, such as:

- Computer game tester
- IT project management – developing computer systems
- Web designing – creating and maintaining web pages
- Multi-media development – working with images, sound, text etc. to create multimedia programs for clients
- Animation – bringing drawings and models to life on screen.

Keep up-to-date!

It will be useful to learn more software packages that are relevant to your job such as:

- Java, C, C++, Assembler and various Artificial Intelligence tools for programmers
- Cool Edit Pro or Logic Audio for audio engineers
- Direct X, Maya or 3ds Max for artists and animators.

Useful contacts

Connexions / Careers Service and UCAS www.ucas.ac.uk
For information on college courses and university degrees, ask your
Connexions / Careers Service.

Skillset www.skillset.org/games
Skillset provides resources for potential game developers in the UK,
including training and qualifications, web pages and a storyboard of game
development processes.

Games Industry Biz www.gamesindustry.biz
This superb site covers all aspects of jobs in the computer games industry.

International Game Developers Association www.igda.org/breakingin
A useful American site suggesting different career paths, featuring developer
profiles and additional resources.

Dare to be Digital www.daretobedigital.com
Check out Dare to be Digital, which is an excellent way to showcase your
skills in the computer games industry.

Blizzard www.blizzard.com/jobopp
Blizzard includes job profiles and 'How to Apply' tips.

Work in Games www.workinmedia.co.uk
A site designed specially for those looking to take their games knowledge
and interest to the next level, regardless of their previous experience.

Further information

As well as the above organisations and websites, specialist magazines are a
good source of computer news and job adverts. A good example of one of
these magazines is *Edge*.

Glossary

aspect – particular feature or part of a whole

avatar – graphical image which represents a person

compromise – to settle a difference by every person giving in a little

concept – general idea of something

copy – words that will be printed or viewed as part of a game, advertisement, newspaper etc.

deduction – reaching a conclusion based on known facts

forum – public place where people can discuss ideas

gameplay – player's overall experience with a computer game: story quality, ease of play, game desirability

genre – particular style, e.g. romance, horror

implicit – unquestioned; implied

interactive – two things working together and reacting to one another

landfill – area of land that is built up in layers by rubbish and then covered in soil

merchandise – goods to be sold

networked – connected by the internet

next-generation – most recent release of a product

platform games – games where the player climbs up and down and leaps from platforms and ledges

prioritise – to list in order of importance

programming – writing and maintaining computer code, which tells a computer what to do

stealth games – games where the player needs to avoid being detected

storyboarding – using a series of illustrations in sequence to visually show a story

texture – how the surface of something feels when touched, e.g. rough, smooth

virtual – situation or setting created by a computer

Index

other titles in the series

PILOT

Elizabeth Dowen   Lisa Thompson

EMERGENCY NURSE

Elizabeth Dowen   Lisa Thompson

TV PRODUCER

Elizabeth Dowen   Lisa Thompson

MAGAZINE EDITOR

Elizabeth Dowen   Lisa Thompson

FORENSIC SCIENTIST

Elizabeth Dowen   Lisa Thompson

MOTOR MECHANIC

Elizabeth Dowen   Lisa Thompson

ANIMATOR

Elizabeth Dowen   Lisa Thompson

BUILDER

Elizabeth Pickard   Lisa Thompson

CHEF

Elizabeth Pickard   Lisa Thompson

SPORTS TRAINER

Elizabeth Dowen   Lisa Thompson

FASHION DESIGNER

Elizabeth Pickard   Lisa Thompson